At The Heart of Your Long Distance Relationship

At The Heart of Your Long Distance Relationship

Love deeply, live fully, and grow closer together from near or far.

Catherine Day

Writers Club Press
San Jose New York Lincoln Shanghai

At The Heart of Your Long Distance Relationship
Love deeply, live fully, and grow closer together from near or far.

Writers Club Press
an imprint of iUniverse, Inc.

For information address:
iUniverse, Inc.
5220 S. 16th St., Suite 200
Lincoln, NE 68512
www.iuniverse.com

Cover Photograph by Robert M. Hayes

ISBN: 0-595-21421-5

Printed in the United States of America

To My Love

Within you, I lose myself

Without you, I find myself

Searching to be lost again

(Anonymous)

Contents

Dedication

While writing this book, our relationships and our lives were forever touched by the tragedy of the September 11th attacks in the USA. Citizens, volunteers, rescue workers, reporters, military; all loved ones, have courageously asked and been asked to find faith, restore peace, feel forgiveness and give love. Though these events may for the moment separate many more of us physically, we are never truly apart.

I dedicate this book to each and every one, of you…

Forward

"Follow your bliss"... Joseph Campbell

Welcome to *At The Heart of Your Long Distance Relationship*. This is for those of you seeking greater understanding, connection and intimacy in your relationship. It is intended to be a heartfelt and helpful guide, offering encouragement, creative ideas and personal activities towards a rewarding long distance relationship experience with your love. It will help you capture what it means to be in a long distance relationship from all levels of your being, physical, emotional, intellectual and spiritual. You can experience what happens when you embark on your relationship of choice including the challenges, rewards, and joys.

At a time when the world we live in yearns for understanding, peace and love, this will help show you where to find it here and now with your partner, no matter where you are. Inside is reassurance and encouragement to keep your love going and keep your partner near even when you are far apart. It's easier than you may think and you have exactly what you need.

Take a closer look at love, communication, trust, friends, and more. Turn the page, reflect on your relationship, be your best, and feel the beautiful world of all that is yours to have with your love. It's within your reach and at the heart of your long distance relationship.

PART I
Having It All

Introduction

We all seek and desire true love and intimacy. At the best of times the relationships that bring us these opportunities are challenging. In a long distance relationship, these challenges are magnified and yet can bring us equal reward and even more.

There are many reasons that we find ourselves in long distance relationships. Sometimes we have chosen them. Sometimes they have chosen us. Situations can change as when our partner moves, goes to college, is relocated or must travel extensively through work, in the armed forces or on business. We may meet someone special at a conference, while on vacation, or even on the inter-net. Love can simply find us, at the most unexpected times in the most unexpected places, no matter where we live. Whatever your situation, it may be that a long distance relationship is simply meant to be. If this is life's plan for you, as it has been presented to me, there are ways we can love and live, find peace and joy and feel intimacy with our partner whether it be from near or far.

The pages that follow explore not only romance but also growth through loving intimacy and by listening to the promptings from the deeper place that resides in us all. Much of this is an extension of my own thoughts, feelings and experiences in my long distance relationships. It is what I have learned over the past years with my partners through our romance, love, communication, humor, spirit and more. All that you want and desire in your relationship is there for you to have and hold.

This will not attempt to analyze the pro's and con's of your relationship choice. Rather, it is for anyone who is currently in a relationship, long distance or right in your own back yard, and has the desire and will to find or rekindle romance and deepen your connectedness and love.

It is an action you can take right now…

1

Forget Logic

When it comes to love and relationships, tradition is out the window and has been for some time. There are thousands upon thousands of long distance relationships. The numbers have likely increased 100,000, 1,000,000, or even more since the advent of the inter-net. They are here and they are here to stay, like it or leave it. With our global economy and mobile lifestyle I would guess that many of us find ourselves separated from our partner often for lengthy periods for reasons personal, educational or career.

If you are reading this book then like me you find yourself in a long distance relationship facing the challenges of physical separation that our not so unique situation poses. If logic dictated, we may not have entered this relationship in the first place, had we known its challenges. Or we may have left it at some point, had we known. Then again, perhaps we would willingly pursue it again, knowing those very same things.

A friend recently asked me why I chose to be in a long distance relationship. Why, I would sacrifice in such a way? I let my inquisitive friend know that it is not about compromise or sacrifice at all. Rather it has led to me finding not only intimate love, but also myself. It is about my being sharing my deepest commitment with another being. I chose this relationship along with my role as a parent and responsibilities of work that required some travel. It is about having it all!

If logic dictated our feelings and actions, and our decisions and choices, I suspect we would be paralyzed much of the time. The facts and figures and equations we would run ourselves through would boggle us like a rat in a maze and halt our ability to be who we really are or to seek what we truly desire in this lifetime. If our choices and decisions were influenced by the opinion of our friends and family we may also not follow our heart. We may never take a relationship risk and we thus keep ourselves from finding a great love.

In a long distance relationship we must especially reach outside our usual thinking and find creative ways to feel our togetherness through the periods of separation. You may be asking yourself how to do this. There are many ways and means to get there. Some are quite logical and some will seem very illogical, wild or "far out", depending on your nature and beliefs. When you try them and experience the results you will see it is well worth it.

I would ask you to begin to open your self first to the ideas, and then open your heart to the feelings, and your soul to the discovery of all that is available to you in the process of finding intimacy with your partner. Don't think about it, just do it. Step onto the train or step away from the track.

2

Romance and Love

"A loving heart is the truest wisdom"... Charles Dickens

A few years ago Tina Turner emotionally sang "What's Love Got To Do With It"? On one hand the answer to this is clear; love has everything to do with it, though exactly what that means often remains something of a mystery.

One of the most difficult things is to look at the difference between romance and love. Are they in fact different? I would say that romance and love are indeed very distinct entities. Most of us believe we want a great romance in our life. Many of us daydream about famous lovers in the movies or in classic novels. Poems and songs are written about romance. What we truly seek may in fact be something different, something more. A great love! An intimate love! A soul mate!

So what makes romance and love so different and how do you get from one to the other? Let's take a moment to examine what is thought to be the differences.

OBSERVATIONS ON ROMANCE AND LOVE

Consider the following observations on romance:

- Romance is about me.

- Romance is "falling in love".

- Romance hits you hard and fast.

- Romance is a feeling.

- Romance is giddy and light-headed.

- Romance has conditions.

- Romance is about sex.

- Romance is temporary.

- Romance is a dramatic.

- Romance is undisciplined.

- Romance means the other person completes us.

- Romance means never being alone.

- Romance is tomorrow.

- Romance means someone to take care of me.

- Romance means the work is over.

- Romance is physical.

- Romance is an escape from reality.

  Now consider the following observations on love:

- Love is not always easy.

- Love is a commitment.

- Love is how we act.

- Love begins with me.

- Love extends outwards to others, "we".

- Love is calm and peaceful.

- Love is not loneliness.

- Love is strong and independent.

- Love must be nurtured.

- Love requires discipline.

- Love is a choice.

- Love changes and grows.

- Love is sex and so much more.

- Love can be painful.

- Love means the work has just begun.

- Love requires conflict and resolution.

- Love has no boundaries.

- Love is the eternity of now.

- Love is spiritual.

- Love is real.

At this point you may be thinking there is too much to consider in being in a relationship at all, romantic or otherwise, let alone a long distance one. So why do we do it? Why be involved in something that would present such challenges? Why go there, stay there, and why would we choose to love from a distance. The answer is simple… because we can.

When one compares the qualities of romance and love, it seems the challenges of a long distance relationship fit quite nicely under the category of love. Perhaps there are challenges in a long distance relationship that bode well in making the heart grow fonder.

Such things as commitment, strength, choice, attention, discipline, pain, boundaries and sex are forced upon us. These things in their availability or lack thereof are painfully obvious from a distance. Thus our opportunities to grow, nurture and experience real love are thrust in our way begging us to discover their gifts.

Look at the qualities of romance and love more closely. Which aspects of each are important in your long distance relationship:

•

•

•

•

•

•

•

3

Keeping Love Alive

"Seduce my mind and you can have my body. Find my soul and I'm yours forever"...
Anonymous

In a long distance relationship we must often quickly suspend our romantic notions because there is little avenue in which they can exist. A long distance relationship may present blessings in disguise to our personal growth and development.

It would surely be foolish to discount all things "romantic" in any relationship. In a long distance relationship, romance is both a valuable and necessary ingredient. The power of romance can keep the door open to loving actions, open communication and deep intimacy between you and your partner.

In a long distance relationship you have many opportunities for romance and romantic gestures. You can let your imagination go, get your creative juices going and make your fantasies come true. I've included some ideas to keep romance alive and deepen your loving connection with your partner. Check those that touch you or that you would like to share with your partner soon. There is also space for you to write out your next romantic actions and loving plans at the end of this chapter and in more detail towards the end of the book. This can be a lot of fun and keeps those loving thoughts flowing.

- Have a treasure chest, scrapbook or photo album containing your precious moments. Keep a decorative box or bag filled with cards, ticket stubs, concert programs, travel brochures, post-cards, dried flowers, and other memories of times with your love.

- Write out a special poem (your own or that of a famous poet) that reflects your feelings and your heart. Keep it in your purse or wallet for easy reference. Look into romantic love poetry at your local bookstore, library or on the inter-net.

- Choosing a poem can be fun as you search for the perfect feeling words for your love. "Shall I compare thee to a summer's day? Thou art more lovely and more temperate"... Shakespeare

- Sing your favorite love song onto an audio or videotape for your partner to hear your voice. Even if you are unsure about your singing voice, be brave, your partner will be thrilled to hear you sing loving words for their ears only. (Think of the Karaoke scene from the movie "My Best Friend's Wedding")!

- Leave surprises like cards, small gifts and notes in your partner's briefcase, gym bag or suitcase. Chocolate kisses, a small piece of jewelry, a sample of your cologne or after shave, a loving note, letter or card, a pocket book, audio tape or anything that will fit, are all nice things to find in unexpected places.

- Plant a "kiss" in your next card, letter or package. When your love opens this card or letter their first thought will be a wonderful visual!

- Remember and honor special dates, happy and sad, like anniversaries, birthdays, deaths of loved ones, promotions and others by sending cards, flowers, chocolates, photos, or more. Always honor those dates and times that are memorable and meaningful to you both whether you are near or far.

- Know the incredible loving power in a surprise! Send your partner flowers or a gift, just because! It's like a soft kiss knowing your love is thinking about you just because you are you.

- Write your love story together and keep a copy close at hand. Describe the wonder of who, what, when, where, why and how of your meeting and getting together as lovers and partners.

- Send virtual cards, hugs and kisses often. It's free! There are countless great online greeting card sites on romance and love, enough to send something every day. Go to your inter-net search engine and look up online greetings.

- Create a booklet of "love" coupons for things like a sensual full body massage, breakfast together, lovemaking, dinner out, a night of pampering; anything that brings you a smile. While making these coupons is fun, by far the best part is redeeming them later with your partner!

- Make a list of your sensual delights. Close your eyes and imagine moments of intimate sharing or making love with your partner. What works for you… soft whispers, moaning, chanting your name, erotic expressions, poetry, music, phone or virtual sex.

- Choose a theme song. Find a tune that expresses the strengths, feelings, and desires that you share and listen to it often for inspiration! This may be the very first tune you heard together or the first song you danced to as a couple or something the words of which simply express how you feel.

- Keep expressive stick-up notes visible at home and at work as reminders of your love. Seeing your partner's "I love you", "I think you're beautiful", "I find you sexy", "I love your body", "I love your smile" can make your day!

- Make a list of your wishes. Things you would love from, or activities you would love to do, with each other. This can range anywhere from a new car, being rich and famous, to a hot date with each other!

- Make a list of the top 10 things that turn you on. Consider all levels of your being and what stimulates you physically, emotionally, intellectually and spiritually.

- Create a document reflecting your commitment to your relationship. Honoring your commitment to communication, trust, and love in this way can be very meaningful.

- List what you will do for and give to each other when you are together next. Draw from your wish lists, sensual delights and things that turn you on.

- Write or talk about the most loving moments in your relationship, so far…

Describe some of the romantic and loving activities you can plan for today, tomorrow and tomorrow after that:

-
-
-
-
-
-
-
-

4

Open Communication

"Never close your lips to those whom have opened your heart"... Charles Dickens

---

We all strive to understand and be understood. Communication is difficult and it is also the pulse of your relationships. It is how we come to know ourselves, and each another and how we come to be loved and love. It is a gift that you cannot see or touch. It is a gift of sharing who you are, your truth. And it is a gift of understanding your partner and their truth. It is the gift of intimacy with your love when you are together or apart.

Real communication takes time and energy and work, the result of which can be unconditional love and acceptance. Good communication nourishes the soul and opens the door to happy long distance relationships and life. It is for you to have an open heart and not be afraid of showing love in everything you say and do.

There are many wonderful resources by way of local seminars, books, tapes, support groups and courses available to you if who wish to build and practice these skills. I have provided a list of tips for open communication. While each is important, I would suggest as a starting point, to check the 10 tips that are most meaningful to you both to act as your guide or rules any time you have something to express or share with your partner.

These are especially important in a long distance relationship because we less often have the ability to make eye contact, to touch or to see each other's expressions and body language. We are unable to see their raised eyebrow, clenched jaw, wink, yawn, crossed arms or smile. Those things that give clues about what may be going on with us. We must therefore sometimes find other ways to reach understanding when we cannot be together.

Share your communication list with your partner and remind yourselves of it often, always keeping in mind your goals of honesty, growth and intimacy in your relationship. Start with your commitment today to make the time to share through open and honest communication.

COMMUNICATION TIPS

- Commit yourself to open and honest communication with your partner. Being committed to communication is the first step towards intimacy with your love.

- Be open and honest at all times about how you feel, don't protect your partner from your truth. A lot of energy goes into holding back your truth and despite your best efforts your partner will sense something is amiss. Chapters 5 and 9 provide more on this important area of communication with your partner.

- Own your own feelings, actions and reactions; they belong to you not your partner. You are the only one responsible for how you feel, act and react to your partner. Be sure not to falsely place blame on your partner for your feelings. Ask your partner what they are feeling. Avoid guessing games.

- Own your own thoughts, they may not shared by your partner. You are the only one responsible for how you think. Be sure not to falsely place blame on your partner for your thoughts. Ask your partner what they are thinking. Avoid guessing games.

- Have the courage to heal though the sharing of your vulnerabilities, fears and imperfections. By allowing yourself to feel your fears and wounds and by sharing them with your partner, you have a wonderful opportunity for closeness, intimacy and true healing. Be sure to ask for and give support while sharing your inner most truth with your love.

- Take the time to hear and to listen without interruption. Your love and connection are always speaking to you if you really hear what is being said by listening with your heart.

- Open your heart and hear with more than your two ears. Listen, touch, and affirm your love while communicating and sharing.

- Accept your partner's feelings and opinions even if you don't share them. Appreciate your love's views and the positive things they bring to your relationship. You may find opportunities for growth!

- Avoid the blame game and lecture traps, and no name-calling! These are all blocks to open communication. Strive to foster a safe and supportive environment for sharing with your love.

- Remain open and non-judgmental no matter what. There is no faster way to end a conversation! There is no need to agree on everything. We all just want to be accepted for who we are and what we believe.

- Reassure your partner when they are sharing their feelings. This provides loving acceptance and encourages resolution.

- Encourage your partner when they are sharing their truth. Once the communication door is open, keep it ajar!

- Be sure to clarify when you don't understand your partner's message. If you are unsure of the intent, confirm what they truly meant with their words or gestures to foster complete understanding.

- Don't read between the lines. Remember the saying, "when you ASSUME, you make an ASS out of U and ME".

- Thank your partner for sharing and for listening. Simple words and actions that are often forgotten. By appreciating their efforts you encourage more from your love the next time and the time after that.

- Write your feelings in a letter or in your journal and share them with your partner. Sometimes it's easier to express your feelings and be sure you are understood in writing.

- Acknowledge and share even those things that are uncomfortable. You will grow by going outside of your comfort zone. Ask for support from your partner when you are unsure.

- Recognize that to apologize when appropriate is strength not weakness. We all make mistakes and what better way to learn.

- Be conciliatory and flexible knowing there is no power in a power struggle. No one wins. Seek a compromise that works for you both whenever possible.

- Consider the impact of your words and decide if it's worth saying. How would you feel hearing these same words? If it doesn't feel good, leave it or rephrase it.

- Silence can be a communication tool or a barrier. Use it appropriately. Prolonged silence can quickly shut down communication with your love. If you need time for yourself explain the parameters and decide when you will deal with the issue.

- Deal with small tensions right away before they become bigger problems. Don't let small molehills turn into insurmountable mountains.

- Use appropriate humor at the appropriate time. No sarcasm or pushing each other's emotional sensitive spots. Chapter 11 provides some helpful hints on humor from near or far.

- Taking pause or "time-outs" are allowed in making your way to understanding as long as it doesn't become a barrier of silence.

- Rather than rehash old problems, work always towards new solutions. Getting stuck on the problem gets you nowhere fast. Look at what needs to be done to improve your situation and move forward.

- Meditate for answers. Chapter 14 shows you ways to find answers in the quiet place of your heart.

- Pray for understanding. Chapter 14 guides you towards better understanding of your love through your spirit.

- Always re-establish contact and end on a loving note. Be sure to find your way to peace before going to bed or parting. Set a positive tone for your next time together whether it is near or far.

Take a moment to evaluate the communication between you and your partner. Make some notes to talk about how you both communicate with the following questions as a guide:

Which of these communication tips do you use?

-

-

-

-

-

-

Are there ways you could improve your communication?

-
-
-
-
-
-

Which of these communication tips could you begin to use?

-
-
-
-
-
-

Are there any things you need to stop doing?

-
-
-
-
-

•

You are never too far away to hear and be heard. Let your voice, your words, and your feelings foster understanding and unlock all that is you. Run towards your love and not away from it with open communication. Work on important decisions together and look for compromise solutions when you see things differently.

I would recommend that any very serious issues that arise in your relationship be communicated in person rather than over the phone or in writing. There is too much opportunity for misunderstanding and it can be tough to mend the fence when you are miles apart on different sides.

Always have the courage to seek help when you are faced with insurmountable impasses or if the going gets too tough.

5

Trust

Trusting your partner in a long distance relationship is essential to loving and feeling joy. There are never guarantees in any relationship and you must be willing to communicate openly and honestly about your fears and vulnerabilities, your wants and needs with your partner.

Our tendency is often to extend a search outside of our self for trust. We may seek in another that quality that will somehow make them "trustworthy" in our eyes. It surprises some people to know that trust is really not about someone else. It begins and resides within you. It requires confidence in yourself and your relationship; enough to express how you feel in specific situations and with certain behaviors.

If you have doubts about your partner's activities or the truth about what they communicate, you can't help but feel a lack of control and unhappy much of the time. If things don't feel right, let your partner know right away. Talk about tough trust issues as they arise. Don't let such feelings build into damaging anger and resentment. If you and your love trust each other you can share your truth and let each other know what is and is not acceptable in your relationship.

Trust yourself enough to have the confidence to talk openly and share your feelings on tough trust issues. Know you deserve a mature and loving relationship based on honesty and faith in one another. The hope is that in sharing your truth you can work through these difficult times both together and apart and feel closer for it. Make use of the communication tips in Chapter 4. If you have trust issues you feel need attention find the right time to discuss them openly with your love. Ask for the understanding and support of your partner during these times.

If you find your partner does not appreciate your concerns or outwardly shows through their behavior that they are not trustworthy, you have another choice. If there is no respect in your relationship from a distance, it is unlikely to be there were you together. If your partner does not value you or take your feelings seriously, communication is compromised and an important part of a loving relationship is lacking. Talk about what you both want to see, hear and feel in your relationship. Set boundaries that you both agree to and by not breaking them, you will instill confidence in the other.

Describe the communication tips and boundaries in behavior that will help you and your partner maintain a healthy trusting relationship:

•

•

•

•

•

•

•

6

Reach Out And Touch

"Emotionally healthy adults (with respect to love) express their total lovingness (emotionally, physically, verbally, lustily) with a particular partner"... from the self-help book, "Be Your Own Therapist"

Within your long-term relationship, it is important to work at your connectedness using all the ways and means available to you. After being with your partner, there is nothing more wonderful than hearing their voice. You can feel their thoughts and feelings and share yours across the miles though verbal expression.

The phone becomes a primary instrument of communication and connection in your long distance relationship. While the expense can add up, I have found there are very reasonable rates through discount phone cards, some as low as one cent a minute, as well as by shopping around the many competitive telephone companies.

Use these times to really hear your love and be heard without distraction. Turn off the stereo, TV and any other outside noise and be present in the moment with your partner. Draw from the list of tips in this chapter and in Chapter 3 to express what is going on during your period of separation and how you feel. These are also opportunities to express your sensual side and to share your wants and desires. Don't be shy! Describe in loving and intimate detail what you will do next time you are together. Don't hold back! Be explicit! Here is an example:

"I hope you had a nice Friday. Now it's time to say take me away! But please let me be there to run your bath water, gently kiss you as I begin to undress you and help you in the tub. I shall bring whatever amenities you need to make it a most pleasant bath time. *wink*. As you finish, I will be there to wrap you in your towel and gently dry you off. Then I will take your hand and lead you to the bedroom where I have folded back the silk sheets and ask you to lay on your stomach. Then I will gently rub some soothing lotion all over your body and begin to give you a most pleasurable relaxing massage. I want you to feel my healing hands all over your body as you begin to drift away in sensual thoughts of what may come next. I will turn you over on your back, gently pressing my body into yours. I lean down and softly kiss you around your neck then move over to your lips. I kiss you softly as you begin to feel the warmth of our bodies generating the heat and passion of wanting each other so that it sends a tingle of passion up and down every inch of your body. Areas of your body begin to pulsate and throb as you become excited, leaving you wanting MORE and MORE and…

Now, what comes next my love? You will find out this evening when you return, *wink*. Hold that thought until we are home. See you soon my love. Stay warm for me. I love you and desire you. Tonight is ours…".

Draw from your own list of sensual delights! Express yourself generously. Go beyond the usual day-to-day details. Be open and honest about your feelings, fears, hopes, and joys. Touch each other's heart deeply and often. The feeling is wonderful!

My partner and I have also found wonderful and fun connection by meeting online in the mornings before work. We are able to lovingly greet the morning together and share our plans for the day.

Most Internet Service Providers give access to a chat site where you can open your own room to talk. Some of the major online sites also provide a downloadable private chat message service. The benefit of these services is that they provide assurance that no other "chatters" will enter your conversations.

You can often personalize your online writing with type shape and color making it more "you". Some services also have the capability to send symbols and pictures reflecting actions, emotions, occasions, flowers, kisses, hugs and much more. This online communication mode can be both fun and surprisingly expressive.

In some ways, this form of communication actually fosters more thought and a deeper awareness as we may feel more freedom in how we express our feelings and interpret those of our partner. It forces us to look creatively at how we can be understood and how we can better understand.

Some Service Providers now also provide the opportunity for free voice messaging and "voice" chat. This means you can hear your partner's voice in notes they have sent and while you chat PC to PC. Check out all the services your inter-net provider is offering today!

Another mode of communication if you have the technology is video or teleconferencing. This provides real time face-to-face or body-to-body connection. You can talk and be heard and see and be seen at the same time. This provides endless possibilities for communication and connection from a distance. If video conferencing facilities or a web cam is available to you, take full advantage. Use your creativity and imagination to communicate fully. Show your love all your good sides, top, bottom, back, front and everything in between.

Sometimes, the old fashioned ways are in fashion once again. The times when my partner and me have shared letters or our journal writings have brought us moments of our deepest understanding and appreciation of the other. In our written thoughtful word, we can shed our masks and fears and open our hearts and bear our souls.

If you are at first intimidated by this, reference the communication tips contained earlier in this chapter. Remain open and non-judgmental when sharing your written words. Listen with your heart. Let yourself experience your partner's truth and they yours. This compassionate sharing can lead to incredible passion. Here is an example…

"Happy Anniversary Honey! These past months spent with you have been incredible. I have discovered so many beautiful things about you that make me love every part of you. I love the simple things like waking up each morning, knowing we can talk about the challenges of our day, giving each other encouragement and support.

I love coming home at night, knowing we can talk about the highs and lows of our day. Sweetheart, you have such a loving and gentle heart, you make it so easy to be in love with you.

You truly bring out the best in me, even when there are days when I don't feel like my best. It is such a comfort to me just knowing you are there. Thank you for letting me know what true love feels like. All of these things make the miles between us seem bearable.

You have touched places deep in my soul. Places I never thought could be touched. You are so beautiful to me, you are everything my heart desires. As my friend, you guide me with your wisdom and grace by sharing your experiences and by listening to mine. By simply giving me your time and patience, by showing your interest, you make me feel that everything I say and do matters; that I matter. As my lover, you touch places in me that bring out my sensuality, and when our bodies are together, I feel our souls are too. The way you simply trace your hands over my skin, the way you leave me breathless with your kisses, makes me want you so much.

There is no other feeling like making love with you. You make all my sexual fantasies become a reality. And after we make love, I feel I am so deep inside you, it makes me just want to hold you and never let you go. I'm filled with such emotion, such joy it makes me want to cry.

I know we have many more months and years to learn and grow together. Somehow it feels like my love for you is without limits, regardless of our distance. I consider every day we share a blessing and look forward to a long future with you. Thank you, for giving me your unconditional love. I pray that we continue to share many more months to come. I love you more than any written words can express. Yours always."

Here are more examples of reaching out to touch your love with some special words...

"Good afternoon sweetheart. Thank you for your beautiful note this morning. I love you so very much. I love you in every way and being with you from now on is what I dream of. I feel all that we share is getting better and deeper each day and each time we are together it becomes clearer and so true. You mean everything to me; you are my love and so much a part of me now. Thank you for just being you and loving me as I love you."

And...

"I wanted to send you a note first thing to start your week, by telling you how much I am in love with you honey. How I long to be with you right now. I have felt such incredible happiness since you came into my life. I just love everything about you. I can feel how wonderful it will be to just sit and watch TV with you, watching our favorite shows and just enjoying time together again. With you babe, I always have a smile in my heart. I want you to be with me always... I hope to see you in a few short weeks. Yours always."

And...

"Thank you for calling today my sweet love... Every word, every feeling, every question you have posed and answered me, I give to you in kind. For I cannot begin to describe the feelings of you deep within me."

Openly express the commitment and love you share. Reassure your partner of the strength of your relationship. Own your thoughts and feelings and share them generously. If words do not flow through you easily, search for heart felt cards and poems that express your feelings and desires. The rewards are well worth the effort to find the right loving message.

How can these modes of communication work for you in your long distance relationship? What forms of connection can you explore now and use in the future:

•

-
-
-
-
-
-
-

7

When You Are Apart

"There is no remedy for love but to love more"... Henry David Thoreau
"To Live is like to love—all reason is against it and all healthy instinct is for it" Samuel But-
ler

There are many dimensions to love and during times of separation from your partner, you will experience many things. Some may not be comfortable. We often associate discomfort or sadness in a negative way, something to be avoided at all cost. Being in love, especially in a long distance relationship, you made the choice to experience the many shades of ecstasy as well as profound sadness. You cannot have one without the other. That is not something to worry over or to fear. It is to live fully! Trust and embrace all of your feelings when you feel them. They are tender and gentle and connect you to your partner and your world in an incredible way.

Those last few minutes before your partner leaves can set the tone for a good part of your time apart. Fill your departing moments with loving communication and gestures. Here are just a few:

- Touch each other often during the day of departure.

- Hold each other in a long warm embrace before you part.

- Hold hands like teenagers!

- Gaze deeply and often into each other's eyes and smile a knowing and loving smile.

- Leave only after a long deep kiss, 10 seconds or longer!

- Validate each other with supportive and loving communication. Review Chapter 4 to reinforce your communication goals.

- Remind each other of the next time you will be together.

- Plan your next communication, when you will talk, write, or meet on the inter-net.

- Be sure to tell your partner to check their briefcase, bag, or pocket for a loving surprise (note, chocolates, a small gift).

- Always say those three simple words… "I love you".

- Make long, passionate love…

By showing your love at the difficult point of separation you leave with feelings of connection to one another that will help you carry on with your usual daily activities. It certainly isn't easy to see them drive away or get onto that plane, train, bus or boat. That last moment when you are each finally out of sight tugs deeply at your heart like few other things.

It is much more enjoyable to end your time together and begin your time apart on a pleasant and energizing tone of togetherness, rather than an energy draining tone of despair, tension, anger or resentment. In doing this, feelings of love and warmth will increase and replace many fears and doubts. Revel in the joy of your love rather than the sadness of parting. Let your smile come through your tears. If this does not come easily to you, the reflective techniques in Chapter 14 may be helpful. Believe in yourself and your relationship and let go of worry.

BRIDGING THE DISTANCE

During those times when your partner is away, there are many things you can do to remain connected to each other. Even simple things can bring you both much joy. Here are activities you can do to bridge the distance when apart. These are fun, easy, romantic and thoughtful.

- Share personalized gifts like a hat or bag with your names, or a calendar, mug or T-shirt with your pictures, to be worn to bed. What better way to remember your love!

- Send your partner your perfumed panties or your T-Shirt with eau de aftershave. Linger in the sensual memories of your last time together.

- Make a video of your activities while apart and share your feelings about them. Stimulate their visual and auditory senses.

- Play love games like "I love you more than…" "The top 5 things I love about you are…" or "I love it when you". A nice reminder of what bonds you and keeps you close.

- Tell your partner your most favorite thing about them. Lest they forget! You can do this verbally, in writing, or physically.

- Send homemade cards, crafts and gifts that help you expend your energy. There is something incredibly intimate about your own personal touch.

- Wake your partner in the morning now and then with a loving phone call. This is a wonderful way to start the day and feel connected to each other. Morning voices are also so deep and sultry!

- Tuck your partner in bed at night now and then with a sensual phone call and pillow talk. Use your best bedroom voice and see where this takes you!

- Be brave and use the inter-net and telephone as a means to "make love" with your partner. Just describe in every detail what you would do with your love, to them, for them all along the way!

- Send email notes to each other often. It's free! Even simple and short communications mean so much and let your partner know you are thinking of them.

- Communicate your sensual delights list from Chapter 3. You can do this in an email, a letter, over the phone or in person.

- Watch the same movie or read the same book. Share afterwards what you felt the message was and the meaning it held for you. Compare notes and learn from each other.

- Wish upon a star together. Remember, it makes no difference where you are! Tell each other what you wish for. Don't let superstition get in the way of sharing your dreams.

- Look out at the moon, the stars, and the planets, while you talk with your love from afar knowing that you are a part of a bigger whole and there are greater things at work in your relationship.

- Choose a celestial body, planet, star or constellation that will be yours and belong to you both. Which one suits your mood? Red, hot Mars, Sexy Venus, Calm Pluto, earthy Earth, the Milky Way?

- Always confirm your love for each other. Nothing soothes more than those three simple words, "I love you". Remember, you can never say or hear these words too often!

- Create routines. Enjoy shared moments of silence or meditation, kiss your partner's picture each night, burn some incense, wish on a star, or pray.

- Share a relationship heart journal. You can keep separate journals or share the same one, taking turns writing the thoughts and feelings from your hearts to share when you are together again or to take with you to remind you of your love each time you are apart. Some ideas to start your writings are described in Chapter 16.

- Even though you are apart, understand there may still be times when you will need to step back. We are after all human and will need moments to ourselves to recharge and to just be.

- Describe to each other over the phone or in an erotic love letter what you will do next time you are together (you can even do this from the next room!). Draw upon your ideas from Chapter 3.

- Play a game of strip poker over the phone or computer! Leave nothing to the imagination. Don't leave out any details as the game progresses! Share colors, textures, sensations along the way. But don't show your cards!

- Be playful and use healthy humor when things get challenging. Having fun is energizing and acts like a magnet when done positively. See Chapter 11 for some fun ideas!

- Send a singing love-o-gram to your partner at work or home. Be serious or be silly, it doesn't matter because it's from you!

- Share your sexual desires and fantasies with each other. How many can you make come true?

- Keep your relationship interesting by varying your method of communication, actions and activities.

- Make the effort to keep in touch in some fashion as often as you can. Even a short note, phone message or conversation can keep you feeling connected and close.

- Feel loveable when you are by yourself as well as together. Trust and confidence in yourself means never feeling insecure in your long distance relationship. Try some of the suggestions in Chapters 8 and 11.

- Send your love a sample of your cologne. This will stimulate sensual and loving memories of you, especially when used with the visualization techniques in Chapter 14.

- Do something a little different and send your love a balloon bouquet. You can be colorful and creative and also include a jar of their favorite chocolates, nuts or jellybeans.

- Send a package of "hugs" and "kisses". You can buy the chocolates or make your own definition of what would symbolize hugs and kisses.

- Never underestimate the pure joy in sending and receiving a perfect single red rose!

Plan some romantic and loving activities you can share while your partner is away:

-

-

-

-

-

-

-

-

8

Taking Care of You

"I'm not afraid of storms, for I'm learning how to sail my ship"... Louisa May Alcott

---

The times when you are apart can also be wonderful opportunities to take time for yourself. I know you may be thinking, "All I have is time with my partner away"! With our rigorous lifestyles of work, parenting and other commitments, there is likely less time for you than you may think.

Respect your differences and those things you share apart from your partner as well as those you hold in common and while together. It's important to give to yourself and do those things that only you can. Focus on you and live your life fully. Here are some ideas to be frivolous and pamper your self when you are separated from your partner:

- Have a hot bubble bath with candlelight and music. Relax in the warmth and glow as you soak away the pressures of your day.

- Get a manicure or pedicure or do your nails. Beautify your extremities with this feel good attention to detail.

- Get a massage. Let a professional therapist work out all the stresses you may be holding in your body.

- Browse in a bookstore, hobby shop or antique shop. Take time to stimulate your visual and creative senses.

- Go for a walk or ride your bicycle. Enjoy the fresh air, the feeling of the wind on your face and the rhythm of your body.

- Go to the gym or work out. Create some feel good endorphins! You'll feel and look great!

- Have coffee or lunch out. Treat yourself to something special. A flavored latte or cappuccino and a healthy snack.

- Leave work early or take a day off for you. Leave the hustle and bustle of 9 to 5 behind and take time to recharge your batteries.

- Have a nap! Refresh your mind, body and spirit with the revitalizing effects of an afternoon siesta.

- Work in your garden. Experience the healing effects of getting back to nature and the beauty of life giving plants.

- See the miracle in simple things. A smile, a touch, a note, a soft breeze, a flock of geese flying in a less than perfect "V".

- Rent that movie you've been longing to watch. What fits your mood? Try a classic, sci-fi, documentary, foreign film or the newest release on the shelf.

- Practice your golf swing. There is no time like the present to improve your favorite game.

- Go window-shopping. Dream of that new suit, power tool, furniture or jewelry.

- Order in a special dinner. Break from the usual and have your favorite take-out or order from a gourmet maitre-de service. Have a glass of sparkling cider or wine and toast to all the good things in your relationship and your life.

- Use your good dishes and crystal. Make every day a special occasion for you.

- Call a friend. Talk with a supportive friend to shake off your cobwebs and give your spirit a lift.

- Get together with a buddy. Some everyday activity and conversation with a focus on light topics can be a welcome change of pace. Catch up on what's going on around you.

- Buy that book you've been longing to read. Go on a mental adventure with a new concept or with interesting characters in unusual and exciting situations.

- Listen to a book on tape. Let a celebrity read your favorite author while you sip on your favorite drink and lounge on the couch or in the sun.

- Have your tarot cards or tea leafs read. Have fun hearing someone's interpretation about you and your future! Take it lightly. You know your truth in your own heart.

- Listen to a relaxation tape and just breath… Become more conscious of your physical and spiritual self by slowing down and taking time to live in the moment.

- Have reflexology done on your feet and toes. Let their fingers do your walking.

- Listen to a personal growth tape. What would you like to find out more about, to do better, or experience. There is always something new to learn!

- Practice random acts of kindness towards others. A good way to feel great. Give of yourself and it will come back to you ten fold.

- Try something new. Go outside your comfort zone! Get meta-physical! Check out a spiritual store for interesting gifts, books and more to deepen your soul.

- Spend a day at the spa. Have a facial, a mud bath, a sauna, and a whirlpool. The works!

- Dim the lights. Relax in the glow of your fireplace or place lighted candles of your favorite scent around the room. Close your eyes, breath and listen to your favorite music.

- Go to church. A good way to reflect and fill your heart and spirit with self-love.

- Have your hair done. One of the simple pleasures in life. Close your eyes and enjoy this personal pampering. Enjoy the easy conversation with your stylist.

- Daydream…

Why put off until tomorrow what you can do today? Plan your next self-care and pampering activities:

-

-

-

-

-

-

-

-

We often ignore the stresses in our lives until they become overwhelming and we are thrown off balance. We can reduce or prevent stress with regular healthy practices. Remember to take care of yourself.

It may seem simple, but a balanced diet is a basic building block. Then there is exercise. Even as little as a few times a week can bring new energy and keep you looking and feeling good. Get plenty of sleep, at least 7 - 8 hours a night. Be sure to practice open communication and share your thoughts and feelings as they arise with your partner. Stay in touch with valued friends and family who give you love, support and joy.

Stimulate your mind by reading, or writing, joining or attending a class. Honor your spirit by visiting and appreciating those things outside of you. Learn and practice relaxation through some form of mediation and prayer. Thoughts on these activities are described in more detail later on.

9

Being Honest And Faithful

"Come live in my heart and pay no rent"... Samuel Lover
"We have enough people who tell it like it is – Now we could use a few who tell it like it can be"... Robert Orben

"Honesty is such a lonely word. Everyone is so untrue", sang Billy Joel. "Honesty is hardly ever heard. And mostly what I need from you". I believe honesty is what we need in a truly intimate relationship. It doesn't have to be lonely or unheard. We all want to be understood, appreciated and loved through open and honest communication and by feeling commitment in our long distance relationship with our partner. I would suggest too that the energy it takes to practice anything less with your love takes more effort than the alternative.

We are all basically good as human beings and know there is right and wrong in society and in our lives. You know when you have been truthful and when you have been dishonest and hurtful. To know your partner is to love them. It is important to own your truth, be willing to hear theirs and to communicate honestly. Holding back or being dishonest can become a burden to your long distance relationship and a barrier to your growth as a couple.

Happiness can always be improved through honesty if you believe in each other and in the love you share. If things do go astray, you can manage them and make them right even during times of separation. How you respond to such challenges in your long distance relationship depends on you. No matter the trials or distance, your relationship can never be broken apart if you view them as opportunities and are honest with your love.

Bring out the best in each other! Let your open communication take you to a new level of sharing and love and appreciation:

- Be supportive when you communicate.

- Consider and be thoughtful of the stresses of your relationship.

- Be upfront and keep your agendas, especially your agenda of love, in the open.

- Always let each other know where you are or how you can be reached. It is a comfort to know you are no further than a call or note away.

- Stay emotionally visible even when you are physically apart.

- Sometimes honesty means admitting you were wrong. Accepting responsibility opens the door to truth and healing of relationship difficulties.

- Focus on all the positive and loving aspects of your relationship and all that it means to you. The effort of honesty is worth it.

- Fill your time with supportive and loving friends and relatives and growing activities that support your commitment.

- Remind yourself of the reasons for your separation and remember your own decision to be in your long distance relationship with your partner.

- Take pride in your strength and honesty with each other and know you will be given everything you need to make it through any difficulties.

- Use your own yardstick to measure your relationship and know in your heart that your love is worth it.

- Your happiness is the best measure of the honesty and trust in your relationship.

- Talk about what is important to you both. Adhere to your boundaries. Do what makes you happy.

- Do what is doable and change what is changeable. Seek improvements and changes in your circumstances if you have options and if it's necessary.

- If things get difficult, remember times of success in the past, and reinforce what works in your relationship when things are going well.

- Find your way to forgiveness if that is what is needed. There is nothing more pure and honest. Remember "forgive" includes the word "give".

- Know that actions speak louder than words. Show your trust and honesty by doing what you say and saying what you do.

- Focus on giving what it is you want. Instead of complaining of any perceived lack, be loving, honest and supportive! It will come right back to you!

- Be sure to reward yourselves when at last you are together again after a period of separation. You met the challenges and are better for it.

- Celebrate alone and with loved ones and celebrate often! You are worth it!

Love is joyous in the truth and in overlooking each other's faults. How you respond to each other and your challenges depends on how you view them. Being unfaithful, no matter what the reason will surely affect your relationship from near or far, at any time. Feeling loving and giving openly and honestly comes from a place of trust and faith. Through trust and faith you will always know what is needed in your relationship and there will be ample space for your love. You will not be missing a thing.

As in every area in your life, you will be presented with obstacles. You may think these are signs that you are in the wrong place with the wrong person. Remember you are here because of your beliefs that it was good and right, because you chose it. Be faithful! Feeling down or being alone doesn't mean you have to be lonely and doesn't justify any indiscretions. If you are expending a lot of energy trying to be faithful or to save an unfaithful relationship, likely the only thing that needs saving is you!

Describe ways you can reinforce the honest and faithful nature of your relationship:

•

•

•

•

•

•

•

•

10

When You Are Together

There is nothing better than that moment when you see your partner drive up in front of your home, or step off the plane, train, bus or boat after a period of separation. The thrill that runs through your body is almost as good as sex! As when your partner departs, those first moments when you are at last together, in each other's arms again, can set the tone for your visit. Make good use of this wonderful event. Don't take anything for granted and don't waste a moment:

- Greet each other with a long, warm embrace and one of your famous long, deep 10- second plus kisses!

- Hold hands like teenagers!

- Be sure to show up! Meet your love after an absence at your very best by looking and smelling great! Touch up your hair, or make-up and lipstick. Put on your love's favorite cologne or after-shave.

- Wear or display something your love has given you as a gift, jewelry, clothing, or tat too!

- Wear your best whatever the occasion casual or formal. Anywhere from your flashy jogging suit, hot jeans, to your sexy new dress and black nylons, to your tailored suit.

- Gaze deeply and often into each other's eyes and smile a knowing and loving smile.

- Validate each other with supportive and loving communication.

- Don't get stuck talking about the subject of any imminent departure.

- Talk about what you've planned during your time together. Stimulate those romantic feelings.

- Share gifts you have for each other, both emotional and material.

- Shower them with your three simple words... "I love you".

- Be attractive emotionally. Generously give and receive loving communication, affirmation and actions when you see your partner.

- Remember that one perfect red rose!

- Get close and breath in the aroma of your lover.

- Make long, passionate love...

Sound familiar? Like your departing moments, your greetings are best filled with feelings of love and warmth. Leave any energy depleting anger, resentment, unsolved problems, worries or fears at the curb at this time. Fully experience the joy of this moment!

You may think that wrapping yourselves up in each other is the only answer when you are at last physically together again. These times are an adrenaline rush, a stimulant high and while incredible and wonderful, they are a part of the real healthy reality. While you will be drawn into these clinches, as with any relationship, it is both important and necessary to continuously nourish the heart and soul of each other.

LOVING THOUGHTS AND ACTIONS

You can keep the juices flowing around these highs while you are together. Here are some thoughts on loving activities when at last you are with your love again:

- Bring gifts home from your travels to personalize and share the time apart. These needn't be extravagant. A bottle of wine, a book, or a card can feel special. Or a favorite candy, chocolate, nuts, jellybeans (my personal favorite), or special blend of coffee.

- Share and celebrate your successes and triumphs and those of the people close to you to reconnect in your lives.

- Remind each other often that no matter what the distance may be between you, you are always loveable and safe.

- Share your goals and dreams often, reminding each other of your future and your commitment.

- Express generously and openly how often you think of each other. It's never too often and it's wonderful to hear.

- Read to each other something that has touched you that week, in the news, a novel, at work, or a spiritual reference. There is an intimate connection in sharing through reading to your love or hearing their voice as they recite something important.

- Plan your next adventure or secret getaway together, whether it's in your own bedroom, at the local campground, the hotel in the next town, or at a new city in a different country.

- Go on the adventure or secret getaway you planned.

- Acknowledge and feel assured that it's okay to be out of sync in any relationship from time to time, even yours. Have the trust and faith to talk about such times.

- Give each other an aromatic sensual massage by candlelight. Be sure there is no time limit. Don't stop with the massage!

- Make good use of your new lingerie or boxer shorts! Show them off and then take them off!

- Do a surprise strip tease before lovemaking. Feel romantic and loving by stimulating your loves imagination!

- Display and wear gifts you've received from your partner. You'll see the appreciation in their expression.

- Have breakfast in bed together. Take turns cooking and pampering the other!

- Stay in bed all day, leaving only for food and water.

- Have an erotic treasure hunt. Lead your partner to the bedroom with a map, a trail of clothes, flower petals or candles, where they will find you waiting…! "X" will definitely mark the spot.

- Savor your favorite meal, wine or dessert together. Feed each other with your fingers, lips and tongue. Who needs utensils?

- Remind your partner of the physical and intellectual attributes you love about them. It feels wonderful to know you are loveable in these ways.

- Remind your partner of the emotional and spiritual qualities you love about them. It feels wonderful to know you are loveable in these ways.

- Draw upon your lists of romantic and loving activities from Chapters 2 and 7.

- Invite your love into the shower and help each other wash those hard to reach places!

- Drop your towel and invite them to join you in bed.

- Focus always on the personal growth or you and your partner.

Don't put off until tomorrow, what you can do today. Take a moment to plan romantic and loving activities while you and your partner are together:

-

-

-

-

-

-

Remember, even when you are together you will occasionally move to different beats. This is natural in any relationship and may be felt more from a distance where you can't be present. Be aware of and understand each other's wants and desires both when you are apart and together. Focus always on the personal growth or you and your partner. Obviously things will arise that you will need to work through whether together or apart. Whatever you do, try to make the most of these times and deal with problems constructively.

11

Humor

"Sometimes your joy is the source of your smile, but sometimes your smile can be the source of your joy"... Thich Nhat Hahn
"Happiness is a perfume you cannot pour on others without getting a few drops on yourself"... Ralph Waldo Emerson

If relationships were all work and no play they would be much less rewarding. Finding humor in day-to-day life and events can keep us light hearted and happy even during the toughest times in our relationship. A smile is worth its weight in gold, and laughter is truly a medicine that helps reduce your stress levels and keep fears down.

Because of our physical distance, we can find ourselves feeling more strain than may be considered usual in a relationship. Having anxiety or feeling grumpy a good part of the time can also definitely act negatively on your long distance experience. Being a bit too serious can start to feel dull and boring. By keeping things light hearted you energize your relationship and are interesting to each other.

Try to have fun on your own and with your love in what you do each day. There is no need to laugh 24 hours a day, just try not to take everything too seriously. Laugh at yourself and with your partner and not at each other's expense. Show each other the lighter side of love. It will lift your spirits at any time. Here are some suggestions to feel the lighter side:

• Search for funny inter-net cards, greetings and cartoons to send to your partner while they are away.

- Phone or write your partner an email or letter about a humorous situation that happened while they were gone.

- Share an embarrassing moment from your past or present. Be supportive as a partner hearing a vulnerable gaffe.

- Mail your partner a funny picture of you, your pets, your friends or family. Write how you felt on the back.

- Slip fun or frivolous cards or small gifts into their briefcase or bag. It's always fun to find something unexpected.

- Smile when you talk and share over the phone. Your love will hear the joy in your voice.

- Watch your favorite comedy show and talk about it afterwards, sharing the humor in the character's lives. Maybe your challenges are pretty small in comparison?

- Leave your partner a funny message on their answering machine. It's a nice way to brighten any day. Be silly and be you. Your partner will love it.

- Be playful! Dance, sing, hug, and kiss from near or far. Foster the fun factor no matter where you are.

- Video tape and send your partner a series of their favorite television comedy. This provides some light entertainment and is especially nice for your love when they are away on serious business.

- Tickle their funny bone with a gift pack including a video or DVD of a light hearted romantic movie release (Sleepless in Seattle, When Harry Met Sally, Pretty Woman or While You Were Sleeping, to name a few. These are sure hits!)

- Call each other by pet names. An intimate and fun way to feel connected as a couple and keep things feeling light hearted.

- Get physical! Nuzzle and tickle often when you are together. A nice reminder to your partner of their physical attractiveness. Everyone craves and loves touch.

- Laugh together for no reason, just because it feels good! Remember a frown is just a smile upside down.

- Order a happy face or heart shaped cake in your love's favorite flavor and have it delivered to their hotel, office or home. Include a light note or humorous card for a shared moment of fun.

- Be physically expressive on your web cam! A little bit of stand-up can go a long way to easing tensions.

- Wink and smile at each other online or especially from across the room or in a crowd. Send that intimate chill down their spine with your knowing look of love.

In what creative ways can you and your partner laugh and have fun:

-

-

-

-

-

-

-

Finding humor and having fun will give your relationship balance. Be creative, make life interesting and you will both keep coming back for more!

12

Circle of Friends

"Love thy neighbor as yourself, but choose your neighborhood"... Louise Beal
"Without the human community one single human being cannot survive"... Dalai Lama

---

When my first important relationship of eleven years came to an end some time ago, I found I was unclear about who I was, what I believed in, who my friends were, and what brought me joy. Much of my time was spent searching for ways to find myself and nourish my soul. This delightful journey of self-discovery continues to this day.

By doing those things you may have put off, and by trying new things that interest you or even challenge you beyond your comfort zone, you are an attractive partner in your wholeness. Don't wait eleven years to find the joy of you. What's stopping you from being yourself and living and breathing fully in your long distance relationship?

Take the time and energy while in your long distance relationship to maintain and build relationships with people you care about and who care about you, doing those things that make you happy. Your true friends are those who care when no one else seems to and keep going when others seem to have given up. Those around you who discourage your relationship are likely not your biggest supporters. Some may even outwardly or subconsciously sabotage your efforts by suggesting you see other people or trying to set you up on dates. If you are committed to the love you share with your partner, consider spending less time with these energy eaters and more time cultivating deep interests and positive supportive friendships.

One of the first things I did was take cooking classes, Chinese and Italian. It was great fun to have a glass of wine, share, and watch someone else cook, while learning in the process.

Other activities I had enjoyed but had only dabbled in were golf and skiing. I took them up with enthusiasm. Golf is a particularly social sport and my partner and me built great friendships through a weekly league in which we could participate on our own or together.

I also had a keen interest in relationships and began attending workshops and groups aimed at personal development and enrichment of mind, body and spirit. I began to meet and develop friendships with people on a new and deeper level than ever before. Many of these friendships continue to this day and are open, honest and most rewarding through our shared interests and experiences. My partner is currently enrolled in adult education courses in the digital media. Between the two of us we always have something interesting to share with each other, and we can't help but be excited about what's next!

Take a moment to think about activities and people that bring you joy and support and love. With your partner away much of the time, be around the positive influences in your life and begin building. Think about the things that make you happy and start something new today. Here are some activities that can help develop ourselves or bring us together with like-minded and hearted people:

- Take a cooking class or two!

- Join or start a book club.

- Join a fitness center, aerobics or yoga class.

- Take a public speaking course.

- Learn a sport or join a team that interests you.

- Join or start a meditation or prayer group.

- Attend workshops on topics you enjoy.

- Take adult education courses to stimulate your mind!

- Join a club that promotes an activity you might enjoy (cards, back-gammon, chess, hiking, biking).

- Start or join a prayer group. Honor your spirit with the like hearted people around you.

- Participate in activities through your local church.

- Volunteer at your community center or for an organization that interests you.

- Join or start a women or men's support group for those in a similar situation.

Not sure where to start? Here are some places you can look for and research ideas:

- At work.

- The College

- The supermarket.

- The bookstore.

- The gym.

- The library.

- Your local paper.

- In magazines.

- Resource Centers.

- Wellness Centers.

- The Community Club.

- The inter-net.

Get to know the people close to you even better and cultivate new friendships by sharing who you are through common interests and activities. Take care of yourself and your own needs and you may put less pressure on your partner, your relationship and the challenge of distance. Fill yourself with the wonder of you! What activities and interests have you longed to undertake? What resources can you check today?

Take a moment to plan what you can do for yourself to live fully now:

-

-

-

-

-

-

-

-

Be a master of your own joy and destiny by finding more meaning in your long distance relationship, including your relationship with yourself. There is enough love between you and your partner to share with you and everyone else in your life! The sky is the limit!

13

Restless Feelings

"Confront your fears, list them, get to know them and only then will you be able to put them aside and move ahead"... Jerry Gillies

It is a natural part of life to be faced with every emotion including the blues, and feeling restless or anxious at times. We are human and these emotions will arise during any relationship and perhaps are more obvious when faced with the challenges of a long distance relationship.

I could tell you to fill your time with all kinds of activities from the previous chapters so you won't have a moment to feel anything, good, bad or indifferent. In the end, a list of distractions won't protect you from your feelings. It's difficult to ignore restlessness or anxiety with mere attempts to divert your attention. While going out, working on a hobby or doing other things are all positive and helpful diversions, pushing your feelings aside or filling them with other activities may not always be the answer and may only delay their inevitable return.

Have the courage to meet all of your emotions head on and you can avoid feeling lonely or needy.

- Accept how you feel and your situation rather than hiding behind an activity or a happy mask.

- Take the time to feel and to meditate for answers. What would really be helpful to you? Chapter 14 provides thoughts and activities for meditation and more.

- Maybe you really need to lend a helping hand to someone else to lift your spirits. The power of giving can fill your heart to overflowing.

- Perhaps giving support to a friend in their time of need will improve your restlessness. To love is to be loved.

- Giving a listening ear to another may be the answer to your own anxiety. Listen and ask for a listening ear in return. Difficulties could actually bring you closer to those around you and bring more intimacy into your relationships.

- Find your own positive energy and turn your feelings into something good!

- Recognize your value and share your gifts of support with your friends, family and community.

- Start or join a support group if you feel a more structured avenue to share and give would be rewarding. Being together with a group of people sharing similar experiences can be very supportive and often fosters personal growth.

- Seek guidance through resources at your local church.

When the emotional going gets tough, do what works to get the results you want. In what ways might you manage stressful relationship feelings you experience from time to time:

-

-

-

-

-

-

-

If your feelings become difficult to manage or keep you from finding joy in day to day living, acknowledge that there is strength in knowing when to ask for guidance and support.

14

Spiritual Connection

"I was always looking outside myself for strength and confidence but it comes from within. It is there all the time"... Anna Freud

---

During times of turmoil within myself or in my relationship I came to find it helpful to find a quiet place for my mind. Racing thoughts and raging hormones can block vision and raise barriers to receiving the answers needed from the heart. When your head has control over your heart and is leading you towards a non-productive thought patterns or non-loving actions, we can try to slow them down and replace them with something more... your spirit.

Go deeper and do things that will further enrich your life and your relationship with your partner. Take the time for you to work on your spirit because you deserve it. Realize that not every impulse and issue you may experience needs to be pursued with your love. You can warm yourself, enrich your soul, and soothe yourself in whatever way works for you. Read, write, meditate, listen to music, or pray. Expand your long distance relationship and feel closer to your partner by exploring your spiritual side. Your love is right there, deep in your heart and soul.

BEING REFLECTIVE

Being reflective can take many forms and mean different things to us. It took me a while to open myself to the very idea of reflective thought through visualization, meditation and prayer. I put up all kinds of roadblocks. It would take too long. It was trivial. It wouldn't help! I didn't know how! While far from being an expert in such practices, I can share my own insights and activities that have worked for me both as an individual and as a partner in my long distance relationships. While some of this may seem unusual, keep your mind open and give it a try. If you don't feel immediate benefits at first, be patient and gentle with yourself. Return to these sections again and practice. As your comfort level increases and you begin to relax you will start receiving clear visualizations, and healing sensations, feelings and insights that will positively influence your long distance experience.

VISUALIZATION

Through visualization, your mind can feel, hear and smell images of those things you would like to experience, like your partner! If you can "see" something or someone through visualization, your body can believe it to be very real. This is one of my personal favorite practices when my partner and me are separated. Being with your partner is no further than visualization away! Here is a suggestion on using the power of your imagination!

Begin by closing your eyes and breathing deeply releasing your tensions and frustrations that have built up. Use your imagination to feel any negative thoughts being drawn from your body and your mind. Feel the healing air curse through your body with each breath. Let each breath bring you a calming energy, slowing your thoughts and then slowing them more. Continue to breath deeply letting your entire body relax.

When your mind and body are resting use your imagination to conjure your desired image, be it smelling your partners scent, hearing their sensual or reassuring voice, feeling their gentle caress, or seeing their warm smile, or more. Remember your list of sensual delights or your erotic love letters and go with your partner as far as your dreams take you. With only a few minutes, this exercise can bring the most wonderful visions and sensations. Relax and open your mind and body to your desired experiences and they will find you anywhere you may be, at home, the Mall, or even at work.

What are the scents, sounds, feelings and sights you would like to experience through visualization. Use your imagination to its fullest, you have nothing to lose!

-

-

-

-

-

-

-

-

MEDITATION

In times of stress, meditation can bring you a sense of calm, clear messages and joy.

There are many styles and depths of meditative practice. Something that has worked for me is what I call "easy meditation" as it involves both the focus on a meditative thought or writing as well as a similar technique to visualization. The idea on meditation is to identify your issue or subject that describes what you are seeking to achieve such as peace, joy, compromise, or forgiveness, etc. Then you focus on that subject in a quiet place without distraction. I have found if I'm unclear about the object of my meditation, that it is sometimes helpful to choose a meditation from a Daily Meditation book or reference.

Find a place that is peaceful and free from distractions where you can be alone. Make yourself comfortable. Focus on the message or read the meditation you have chosen to yourself, pausing after each word or sentence. Let the words drift through you. Take them into your head and let them flow downwards through you and into your heart. Feel them inside you.

Repeat this exercise and let the meaning rest within you. What message do you hear? Let your mind slow its pace and feel the healing. Sit in silence and roll the feelings around until you begin to hear the lesson being presented to you. Embrace the message. Be willing to accept its value and open your heart knowing you deserve love and support from the Universe. Let your fears go, feel them dissolving within you. Allow the difficult moment to soften and pass so the answer can replace it. Breathe deeply, and trust that your choices will lead you to joy, let the love extend from you to your partner and into the world. You need not struggle any longer. The answer is never more than a meditation away.

Is there a situation you may be experiencing that could be healed through meditative acceptance?

●

●

●

●

●

●

●

●

PRAYER

Prayer is a gift. Delight in it! Through prayer comes a place where we can open our hearts and our slightest word or sound will be heard. For me, what I think is how I pray; my thoughts are my prayers. This means I can pray and be heard at any time in any place. Pray in whatever way feels right for you in your heart. Believe what you want to see and it will present itself to you (though it may not always in the form you expect!).

Look at your partner with love and not for love. See that they are loveable and focus on being loving in return. If you see love and give love it will be before you and will come back to you. Being loving is simply being your true self. Be true to you, be tolerant, be forgiving, and be creative. Be positive by focusing on all that is good in your relationship and in your life.

Ask the Universe to show you and your partner the way to your hearts and the way home. It may be easier than you think. You can discover everything that you seek. We never ask for too much! We ask for too little! It's never wrong to ask, the Universe already knows what you need. Open yourself to a higher good being made available to you. Pray for understanding. Receive it. Feel it's healing. There is no need to struggle in darkness when there is only light.

Sometimes it's hard to find the words to say and pray for what is in your heart. We may feel hurried or distracted. The thoughts get stuck. What better time to rest in prayer. At such times, I find the "The Serenity Prayer" by Reinhold Niebuhr can be a good place to start. I've included the touching words of this prayer here for you. The message of this general prayer also seems to fit so well with the challenges of long distance love. Revisit the words often. You can find new understanding and meaning each time you take them into your heart. For at the heart of our relationship lays all these things, courage, acceptance, love, peace, trust, and happiness. Amen.

Though understanding need never be more than a prayer away, do not hesitate to ask for help and seek professional guidance if your barriers are overwhelming. We are human and the answers to our challenges are not always clear. Know that there is true strength in acknowledging our humanness and by asking for help and support to get through difficult times.

The Serenity Prayer

God grant me the serenity
to accept the things I cannot change;
courage to change the things I can;
and wisdom to know the difference.
Living one day at a time;
Enjoying one moment at a time;
Accepting hardships as the pathway to peace;
Taking, as He did, this sinful world
as it is, not as I would have it;
Trusting that He will make all things right
if I surrender to His Will;
That I may be reasonably happy in this life
and supremely happy with Him
Forever in the next.

Reinhold Niebuhr

How might prayer bring you a sense of peace and joy in your relationship today though better understanding and acceptance?

-
-
-
-

-

-

-

-

While many of your deepest thoughts, feelings and desires belong to you and you alone, do consider sharing some of your reflections, visualizations, meditations and prayers with your love. Even sharing visualizations as simple as holding your love's hand while driving home from work can open the door to more intimate communication and connection. But don't stop there! Share your more erotic visualizations, over the phone or in writing. Share also the things for which you've asked for more understanding or guidance through meditation or prayer. These activities can bring deep feelings of closeness no matter how far apart you may be. Do what feels right for you in your heart.

15

When All Is Said

"The course of true love never did run smooth"... William Shakespeare

---

We will come to impasses in our relationships. We will get stuck, feel angry or hurt. There will be times when we feel wronged by our partner, life seems unfair and all seems hopeless. There will always be those times when things feel too difficult and we cannot seem to resolve our issues, the ones that keep coming back over and over again no matter what we do. These times can be discouraging in any relationship. In a long distance relationship they are even more glaring. This is when we can bring the relationship and our selves to a new and different level. These are the challenges and things we must surrender through compassion and acceptance. This is when we are asked to consider our partner and our selves in a more realistic light.

When these times arise, it may be time to let go. Not of your partner, but of your ideas of what is right and wrong, good and bad, pain and pleasure. This is where you will see miracles take place. This is where your real power and trust is felt. It is the power and trust you will find in faith. Know that it is only in your state of vulnerability where true understanding and answers to your tough questions can be heard. The answer may be that you need to initiate that long held discussion. Perhaps you need to make that decision you've been putting off. Or maybe it's time to express your needs, communicate your truth or hear those of your partner. This is where you listen to your instincts and trust in them to do whatever it takes to be victorious.

In the end, the truth is you really have no control over your relationships or the people in them. The best you can do is to fill yourself though giving and receiving love. It isn't up to you to change your relationship, your partner, anyone or anything. Release the gifts your partner has given you, let them come through you and out of you and wait for their return.

All that matters is that you have learned and grown in the process of your relationship; expect nothing in return. In a long distance relationship this truly requires a leap of faith and an act of courage. Remember The Serenity Prayer? If it is meant to be you will be rewarded by loves gift back to you. If it is not meant to be, consider separating if it seems the best action to take and go to bed simply knowing and finding comfort in the very miracle of your own giving.

What things are important to discuss with your partner to help maintain your healthy relationship:

•

•

•

•

•

•

•

•

PART II
Your Heart Journal

16

In Your Own Words

"Where there is love, there is life"... Mahatma Gandhi

This section is dedicated to your own personal thoughts and writings. These pages provide you with the opportunity to express your own thoughts, feelings and ideas in more detail on some of the topics described in this book. They can serve as the beginning to a daily or weekly journal activity of your heart or simply as a quick reference and reminder about romantic and loving things important to you and your partner.

WRITINGS FROM YOUR HEART

Take your time and give each of the topics thoughtful consideration. Have fun developing things like your love story, sensual delights, and wish lists. Involve your partner and share feelings while you are exploring what you both enjoy. Use this as a further opportunity towards open loving communication, deepening your understanding and as a reminder of the reasons you are in love and together.

Here is a brief review of the topics selected for you to expand upon in the pages that follow:

• In our relationship romance and love are about... Go back to Chapters 2 and 3 and describe what romance and love mean between you and your love. What romantic and loving beliefs contribute to the success of your relationship and keep you together.

- The words to our special love poem. Write out the love poem that bonds you as a couple. Describe the reason you chose this poem. What does it mean to you? How does it touch your heart and soul?

- The words to our theme song. Write out the words to the song that you share together. Describe how this came to be "your" song. Where were you when this song became "yours". What were you doing at the time? How does it feel each time you hear its melody and lyrics?

- Our love story. How did you and your love meet and become a couple. Was it happy, sad, funny, a little bit of everything? Who pursued whom? What was your first date? Get sentimental and descriptive.

- The most loving moments in our relationship, so far... capture those wonderful times that reflect your most special memories through romantic and sentimental sharing.

- A letter of commitment to our love. Write about all the reasons you are together and will stay together. What qualities in your relationship bring you peace, faith, strength, hope and love.

- A list of my sensual delights. Go into detail on what brings you pleasure and share this with your partner. Use the opportunity to communicate, visualize, and embrace your physical side.

- A list of my partner's sensual delights. Do the same exercise to embrace your partner's physical side.

- The Top 5 things we love about each other. Writing these out is a physical reminder of the love you share. Write them, recite them, and remind each other of them. And remember, you don't have to stop at 5! This list can go on and on...

- If I could have 10 wishes. What would you want with your partner, in life, in love, in body, in mind, and in spirit. Let the genie in the lamp give you not just 3 but 10 wishes to come true!

- If my partner could have 10 wishes. Do the same exercise with your partner. Find out what they wish for in this lifetime. How many can you both make come true!

- The top 10 things that turn me on! Don't hold back. Share the 4 areas of your humanness: physical, emotional, intellectual, spiritual.

- The top 10 things that turn my partner on! Need I say more?

- Our top 10 communication rules. How do these work to keep you close? Reinforce the things you are doing well and how these help you meet your unique challenges.

- A love letter to my partner. "How do I love thee, let me count the ways"... Share your hopes and dreams.

- My Partner and I have fun and humor in... Describe the things, activities and qualities in your love that bring you joy and laughter. Work on this together and have fun.

- Our fears, strengths, and dreams. By sharing these you become vulnerable and by doing so you become closer. Sharing even the things we fear provides an opportunity for loving reassurance and a deeper connection. There is strength in vulnerability.

- A prayer for us. What do you pray for in your relationship, for your love, for you, for all? Write these things out and keep them close to your heart. Tell your love how you feel and what you pray for.

- A list of what we will do for and give to each other when we are together next. Let your imagination take you to every corner of your being.

- Other thoughts and feelings about our relationship. What else is important to you, to your relationship? What thoughts and feelings have arisen during these exercises? What do I need to share with my love today, tomorrow and always? How will I do this? The beginning may be as simple as saying… "I love you".

Now take some time alone or with your love. Use this as a chance to deeply connect and share openly and lovingly on all levels. Ponder these topics and questions and begin your "Heart Journal" in the space provided in the following pages. Feel them in your body and mind and let them move your soul.

In Our Relationship Romance And Love Are About:

_____

_____

_____

_____

_____

_____

_____

_____

_____

_____

_____

_____

_____

_____

_____
_____
_____
_____
_____
_____
_____
_____
_____
_____

The Words To Our Special Love Poem Are:

_____
_____
_____
_____
_____
_____
_____
_____
_____
_____
_____
_____
_____
_____
_____
_____
_____
_____

_____

_____

_____

_____

_____

_____

_____

_____

The Words To Our Theme Song Are:

_____

_____

_____

_____

_____

_____

_____

_____

_____

_____

_____

_____

_____

_____

_____

_____

_____

_____

_____

_____

_____

_____

_____

Our Love Story Is:

_____

_____

_____

_____

_____

_____

_____

_____

_____

_____

_____

_____

_____

_____

_____

_____

_____

_____

_____

_____

_____

_____

_____

_____

The Most Loving Moments in Our Relationship So Far:

_____
_____
_____
_____
_____
_____
_____
_____
_____
_____
_____
_____
_____
_____
_____
_____
_____
_____
_____
_____
_____
_____
_____
_____
_____

A Letter of Commitment to Our Love:

_____

_____

_____

_____

_____

_____

_____

_____

_____

_____

_____

_____

_____

_____

_____

_____

_____

_____

_____

_____

_____

_____

_____

_____

_____

_____

A List of My Sensual Delights:

_____

_____

A List Of My Partner's Sensual Delights:

_____
_____
_____
_____
_____
_____
_____
_____
_____
_____
_____
_____
_____
_____
_____
_____
_____
_____
_____
_____

The Top 5 Things We Love About Each Other Are:

_____
_____
_____
_____
_____
_____
_____

_____
_____
_____
_____
_____
_____
_____
_____
_____
_____
_____
_____
_____
_____
_____
_____
_____

If I Could Have 10 Wishes They Would Be:

_____
_____
_____
_____
_____
_____
_____
_____
_____
_____

_____

_____

_____

_____

_____

_____

_____

_____

_____

_____

_____

_____

_____

_____

_____

_____

If My Partner Could Have 10 Wishes They Would Be:

_____

_____

_____

_____

_____

_____

_____

_____

_____

_____

_____

_____

_____

_____

_____

_____

_____

_____

_____

_____

_____

_____

_____

_____

_____

_____

The Top 10 Things That Turn Me On (physically, emotionally, intellectually, spiritually):

_____

_____

_____

_____

_____

_____

_____

_____

_____

_____

_____

_____

_____

_____

_____

_____

_____
_____
_____
_____
_____
_____
_____
_____
_____
_____

The Top 10 Things That Turn My Partner On (physically, emotionally, intellectually, spiritually):

_____
_____
_____
_____
_____
_____
_____
_____
_____
_____
_____
_____
_____
_____
_____
_____
_____

_____

_____

_____

_____

_____

_____

_____

_____

Our Top 10 Communication Rules:

_____

_____

_____

_____

_____

_____

_____

_____

_____

_____

_____

_____

_____

_____

_____

_____

_____

_____

_____

_____

_____
_____
_____
_____
_____

A Love Letter To My Partner:
_____
_____
_____
_____
_____
_____
_____
_____
_____
_____
_____
_____
_____
_____
_____
_____
_____
_____
_____
_____
_____
_____
_____
_____
_____

_____

_____

My Partner And I Have Fun And Find Humor In:

_____

_____

_____

_____

_____

_____

_____

_____

_____

_____

_____

_____

_____

_____

_____

_____

_____

_____

_____

_____

_____

_____

_____

_____

Our Fears, Strengths And Dreams Are:

_____

_____

_____

_____

_____

_____

_____

_____

_____

_____

_____

_____

_____

_____

_____

_____

_____

_____

_____

_____

_____

_____

_____

_____

_____

_____

_____

_____

A Prayer For Us And Our Relationship Is:

_____

_____

_____
_____
_____
_____
_____
_____
_____
_____
_____
_____
_____
_____
_____
_____
_____
_____
_____
_____
_____
_____
_____
_____
_____
_____
_____
_____

A List Of What We Will Do For And Give To Each Other When We Are Together Next:

_____
_____
_____
_____

_____
_____
_____
_____
_____
_____
_____
_____
_____
_____
_____
_____
_____
_____
_____
_____
_____
_____
_____
_____
_____
_____

Other Thoughts And Feelings About Our Relationship:

_____
_____
_____
_____
_____
_____

_____
_____
_____
_____
_____
_____
_____
_____
_____
_____
_____
_____
_____
_____
_____
_____
_____
_____
_____
_____

Other Thoughts And Feelings About Our Relationship:

_____
_____
_____
_____
_____
_____
_____
_____
_____

_____

_____

_____

_____

_____

_____

_____

_____

_____

_____

_____

_____

_____

_____

_____

_____

_____

_____

_____

PART III
Today and Tomorrow

17

The Future Of Love

One of the most important things in your long distance relationship is to talk about and plan for your future. What better way to start and end each day. My partner and me have found there is joy and peace in knowing what we believe will come next. It keeps us close and gives ongoing connection. There is much fun and enjoyment in planning your next romantic gesture, your next loving activity, your next open communication, your next pampering, your next prayer, your next vacation, and the next all important time together.

It is my hope and prayer for all of us in a long distance relationship that our common goal of being together with your partner in every way will come true. Through our practical understanding, appreciation, love, faith and belief we can realize our dream. That is what makes our hearts smile and our souls dance. Here are some more loving thoughts to hold in your heart and keep you and your love close:

- You are always close at heart. Look no further than inside yourself and the love you share will be right there, deep within you. You need not go anywhere.

- There are forces bigger than you and your partner at work, watching over you, keeping you and your love safe.

- Your path, bumps and all, lead only to your love.

- Love is always light. Only fear is heavy.

- Practice being grateful for all that you do have together.

- Give yourself credit and trust in your relationship. It is hard work no matter where you may be and you're doing great!

- Love completely. If you only give 50% and you are waiting for your partner to give the other 50% in return, you only have half of a full relationship.

- We do difficult things each and every day. The impossible just takes a little longer. Patience is a virtue!

I'd like to leave you with the words of Corinthians on Love, for I believe it speaks to the heart and soul of those in a long distance relationship and any important relationships. It is about loving deeply, honestly and fully, with maturity, trust, and self-acceptance. It is ultimately about our courage to be true to our self and others thus freeing us to receive and give true love. Read the words and take them in. Feel them and cherish the feelings they provoke. Trust in their truth and in yours knowing always that:

- Love is always kind

- Love is happy in the truth.

- Love is gracious, generous, flexible, overlooking the others faults.

- Love is open and believes the best in each other.

- Love is always mature and strong.

- Love is infinite with enough to share.

- Love has the strength and power to wait.

• Love has the ability to endure hurt and pain.

• Love triumphs over all!

I hope the ideas and activities here as well as your own thoughts and writings along the way have been helpful. For a love that is deep and true is yours right here and right now. It doesn't matter where you live or where your love may be at this moment. You can be together in every moment at the heart of you long distance relationship.

All you need do is ask…

Love is patient;
Love is kind;
Love is not envious or boastful or arrogant or rude.
It does not insist on its own way; it is not irritable or resentful; it does not rejoice in wrongdoing, but rejoices in the truth.
It bears all things, believes all things, hopes all things, endures all things.
Love never ends.
But as for prophecies, they will come to an end; as for tongues, they will cease; as for knowledge, it will come to an end.
For we know only in part, and we prophesy only in part; but when the complete comes, the partial will come to an end.
When I was a child, I spoke like a child, I thought like a child, I reasoned like a child; when I became an adult, I put an end to childish ways.
For now we see in a mirror, dimly, but then we will see face to face.
Now I know only in part; then I will know fully, even as I have been fully known.
And now faith, hope, and love abide, these three; and the greatest of these is love.

(Corinthians 13:1-13)

Epilogue

※

After September 11, 2001

"There is no end. There is no beginning. There is only the infinite passion of life"... Federico Fellini

---

As I was writing these very pages, I sat in horror as the events of September 11th unfolded before our eyes. My partner had called me on that morning and we watched together as the first and then second beautiful silver jet hit the magnificent twin towers in New York City. The City that never sleeps was awakened to a jarring unthinkable nightmare. We sat together in silence knowing that what was happening would forever change us and our relationship and our lives.

The fear that struck our hearts was like nothing we had ever experienced before. I sheltered my daughter from the barrage of newscasts and reassured her that we were safe and loved, even when I had doubts of what may happen next. We could do nothing but let the shock waves we were feeling ripple through us.

Thankfully, we have learned that our relatives and friends living and working in NYC are safe. We acknowledged, that were it not for the grace of God, we could also be.

Our deepest sympathy, love and heartfelt prayers are with everyone touched by this immense tragedy. There is no question that we have all been touched in some way and our lives and relationships are forever changed.

After the shock and disbelief of the most unthinkable devastation, came some of the biggest challenges to our long distance relationship. Fears that we were both afraid to acknowledge and questions that we were both afraid to ask arose at once. All made even more daunting as we live in different countries. We have been humbled in our expectations in a way we never imagined possible.

We talked about the meaning to each of us and looked at what it may mean to us as a couple. The hurdles that we faced in our long distance relationship in the normal course of our lives now seemed minute in comparison to what we now face. We are mourning those losses and the losses to what we now see as a past carefree life.

Through it all, one thing became clear to us, the power of our love. We felt a knowing that our long distance relationship would survive any and all challenges. We realized that if we changed our feelings and behaviors because of recent world events, that terror and fear would have triumphed over love and joy. We knew without doubt that nothing and no one would come between us, with the exception of us. We strengthened our resolve towards our long distance relationship challenges and became more committed to one another in spite of our obstacles.

My partner and I now do even more of the things described in these pages, knowing anything can change at any moment. We talk more and more intimately. We share more and in more heartfelt ways. We live for today and plan for tomorrow. We laugh more about more simple things. We take better care of ourselves and of each other. We generously share our feelings and our dreams. We touch each other through our beliefs and our spirit.

We continue to travel to be together physically. We have learned through this, to never take things for granted and to always appreciate the time we do have. We are about here and now, not about what was or what may be.

Stop for a moment and consider the things you regret. What are they? What are you trying to wish away or wish for? Regrets are born of the things we did not do or did not say, rather than those we did. Have no regrets.

We trust that we will be given the means and have faith that we will be shown the way to meet whatever challenges face us in our relationship. Our relationship is stronger and more intimate than it has ever been. When we feel darkness, we will search for the light side and the blessing it brings.

Love is the ultimate intimate relationship between two people that grows from our heart and soul. It is alive and fills the distance between us. We can and will love each other, no matter where we may be and no matter what may happen around us.

Love is the one constant we all share.

The End

and

The Beginning

About the Author

Cat is in her second long distance relationship. She is a health care practitioner and President of a local Professional Association with a long time interest in communication and connection. Cat currently works as a Corporate Manager and lives happily in her long distance relationship and with her daughter and two cats in Canada.

"At the Heart of Your Long Distance Relationship"

This book is a heartfelt and helpful guide, offering encouragement, creative ideas and activities towards greater understanding and intimacy with your partner. It is for anyone with the desire and will to find or rekindle romance and deepen your connectedness and love, long distance or in your own back yard. It is an action you can take, right
now…

Includes:
Inspirational quotes! Personal writing topics!
Over 250 ideas on communication, romance, love
and more!!!

Website:
http://ldromance.tripod.com/attheheartofyourldr

0-595-21421-5

www.ingramcontent.com/pod-product-compliance
Lightning Source LLC
Chambersburg PA
CBHW020255290526
45784CB00003B/1262